Gluten and Dairy-free (
101 Easy Family Recipes
for Busy People on a Budget

by Alissa Noel Grey
Text copyright(c)2022 Alissa Noel Grey

All rights reserved. No part of this publication may be reproduced, distributed, or transmitted in any form or by any means, including photocopying, recording, or other electronic or mechanical methods, without the prior written permission of the publisher, except in the case of brief quotations embodied in critical reviews and certain other noncommercial uses permitted by copyright law

Although every precaution has been taken to verify the accuracy of the information contained herein, the author and publisher assume no responsibility for any errors or omissions. No liability is assumed for damages that may result from the use of information contained within.

Table of Contents

Gluten and Dairy-free Recipes for Busy People on a Budget — 6

Salad and Side Dish Recipes — 9

Vitamin Chicken Salad — 10

Chicken, Lettuce and Avocado Salad — 11

Tomato, Chicken and Arugula Salad — 12

Mashed Avocado and Chicken Salad — 13

Easy Chicken and Egg Salad — 14

Beef, Spinach and Avocado Salad — 15

Steak Salad with Arugula and Avocado — 16

Mediterranean Beef Salad — 17

Ground Beef Salad with Creamy Avocado Dressing — 18

Warm Leek and Sweet Potato Salad — 20

Beet Salad with Walnuts — 21

Warm Beet and Lentil Salad — 22

Avocado, Black Bean and Red Pepper Salad — 23

Easy Artichoke and Bean Salad — 24

Cabbage, Carrots and Turnip Salad — 25

Roasted Vegetable Salad — 26

Mediterranean Avocado Salad — 27

Spinach and Asparagus Salad — 28

Pumpkin and Spinach Salad — 29

Easy Chickpea Salad — 31

Chickpea and Avocado Salad — 32

Homemade Hummus — 33

Chickpea and Avocado Hummus — 34

Soup Recipes — 35

Mediterranean Chicken Soup	36
Chicken and Butternut Squash Soup	37
Chicken and Sweet Potato Soup	38
Creamy Chicken Soup	39
Broccoli and Chicken Soup	40
Beef and Vegetable Soup	41
Ground Beef and Vegetable Minestrone	42
Italian Meatball Soup	43
Rich Meatball Soup	44
Celery, Apple and Carrot Soup	45
Easy Vegetable Soup	46
Curried Parsnip Soup	47
Mushroom and Kale Soup	48
Spinach Soup	49
Mediterranean Lentil Soup	50
Carrot and Chickpea Soup	51
Minted Pea Soup	52
Main Dish Recipes	53
Walnut Pesto Stuffed Chicken	54
Chicken with Olive Paste	55
Mediterranean Chicken Stew	56
Chicken Drumstick Casserole	57
Hunter Style Chicken	58
Healthy Chicken Meatballs	59
Bacon Wrapped Chicken Breasts	61
Healthy Chicken Dippers	62
Spicy Mustard Chicken	63

Garlic Chicken	64
Chicken Puttanesca	65
Grilled Chicken with Herbs	67
Greek Style Chicken Skewers	68
Chicken and Chickpea Casserole	69
Greek Chicken Casserole	70
Chicken and Lentil Stew	71
Chicken with Mustard Lentils and Spinach	72
Stephanie's Meatloaf	73
Spicy Burgers and Vegetables	74
Ground Beef and Brussels Sprouts	76
Roast Beef with Quince, Parsnips and Carrots	77
Eggplant With Ground Beef	78
Steak with Olives and Mushrooms	80
Mediterranean Beef Casserole	81
Beef with Melting Onions	82
Beef with Mushrooms	83
Lamb Asparagus Stew	84
Spring Lamb Stew	85
Pork Skewers	86
Salmon Kebabs	87
Mediterranean Baked Salmon	88
Almond and Oregano Crusted Fish Fillets	89
Easy Coconut Fish Curry	90
Lamb Tagine with Green Olives and Lemon	91
Beef Tagine with Sweet Potatoes	93
Ground Beef and Cabbage Casserole	95

Ground Beef and Lentil Casserole	96
Baked Cauliflower	97
Maple Roast Parsnip with Pear and Sage	98
Balsamic Roasted Carrots and Baby Onions	99
Hearty Chicken Spinach Frittata	100
Chicken and Mushroom Frittata	101
Zucchini and Buckwheat Stew	102
Power Buckwheat Stew	103
Curried Buckwheat with Raisins and Apples	104
Quick Buckwheat Chili	105
Eggplant and Chickpea Stew	106
Spicy Chickpea and Spinach Stew	107
Moroccan Chickpea Stew	108
Baked Falafels	110
Chickpea, Rice and Mushroom Stew	111
Chickpea, Leek and Olive Stew	112
Easy Homemade Baked Beans	113
Baked Bean and Rice Casserole	114
Green Pea and Rice Casserole	115
Breakfast and Dessert Recipes	116
Hearty Quinoa and Spinach Breakfast Casserole	117
Applesauce Pancakes	118
Super Easy Blueberry Pancakes	119
Raspberry Muffins	120
Raw Brownie Bites	121
Zucchini Breakfast Smoothie	122

Gluten and Dairy-free Recipes for Busy People on a Budget

There are tons of reasons for choosing an anti-inflammatory gluten-free and dairy-free diet. Some choose to do so because of a dairy allergy or wheat intolerance, while for others it's in order to improve their general health and well-being. Gluten and dairy intolerances usually show with adverse digestive issues such as bloating, gas, diarrhea, cramps, and a myriad of other symptoms like irritability, depression, brain fog, acne or eczema. All these will disappear after eliminating gluten and dairy temporarily from your diet and then reappear when you reintroduce them.

If you are on the edge of going gluten and dairy-free, you will be surprised at the positive side effects of this diet. Even people that do not suffer from gluten or lactose sensitivity, report feeling less lethargic and more energized after eliminating gluten and dairy from their diet. As an added bonus, due to the lack of processed grains, a lot of people also lose weight.

Going gluten and dairy-free for any reason will require a good bit of planning but fortunately can be also really simple as the majority of whole foods are naturally gluten and dairy-free. You just have to focus on incorporating them in your everyday cooking. All vegetables and fruit, rice and quinoa, fresh unprocessed meat, poultry, and seafood, legumes, nuts, seeds, and plain tofu are great anti-inflammatory foods. Counterintuitively, eggs are also gluten and dairy-free. Overall, the list is fairly long, and does not even begin to cover the gluten-free and dairy-free substitute foods that are out there these days.

Following a gluten and dairy-free diet doesn't have to feel as intimidating as it might sound. In fact, with the right recipes you won't think twice about missing either! Planning simple, home cooked meals and choosing naturally gluten-free and dairy-free whole foods will make your transition to allergy and inflammation free lifestyle much easier. Here are some easy-to-make delicious recipes the whole family will enjoy!

Foods You Can Enjoy While Following a Gluten and Dairy-free Diet

- Meat - beef, veal, pork, lamb, rabbit, chicken, turkey, duck
- Fish and shellfish – sardines, salmon, tuna, halibut, sole, trout, bass, haddock, turbot, tilapia, cod, mackerel, anchovy, herring, crab, lobster, shrimps, scallops, clams, oysters, mussels.
- Eggs - hen eggs, duck eggs, goose eggs.
- Fats - olive oil, coconut oil, avocado oil, veal fat, lamb fat, nut butters, nut oils.
- Mushrooms - button mushrooms, oyster mushrooms, portobello, shiitake, chanterelle, crimini, porcini.
- Vegetables - all vegetables are gluten and dairy-free. Potatoes, tomatoes, bell peppers, cucumbers, celery, onions, garlic, leeks, green onions, eggplants, cauliflower, broccoli, asparagus, cabbage, Brussels sprouts, artichokes, okra, avocados, lettuce, spinach, collard greens, kale, beet greens, mustard greens, Swiss chard, turnip greens, watercress, endive, arugula, radicchio, chicory, bok choy, carrots, beetroot, turnips, parsnips, sweet potatoes, radishes, artichokes.
- Rice - all rice in its natural form is gluten-free. This includes white rice, brown rice, wild rice and also rice flour.
- Legumes - beans, lentils, chickpeas, green peas, mange tout, sugar snap peas
- Winter and Summer Squashes – pumpkin, butternut squash, buttercup squash, zucchini, yellow summer squash.
- Fruit - all fruit are gluten and dairy free. Apples, pears, peaches, nectarines, apricots, cherries, bananas, oranges, tangerines, grapefruit, strawberries, raspberries,

cranberries, blueberries, blackberries, plums, pomegranates, pineapple, papaya, grapes, cantaloupe, water melon, honeydew melon, kiwis, lemon, lime, lychees, mango, coconut, figs, dates.
- Nuts and Seeds - quinoa, sunflower seeds, pumpkin seeds, walnuts, pecans, pine nuts, macadamia, chestnuts, cashews, almonds, flaxseed, sesame seeds, hazelnuts, pistachios, Brazil nuts.
- Herbs and spices - parsley, dill, oregano, rosemary, basil, thyme, bay leaves, mint, chives, tarragon, sage, coriander, black pepper, paprika, summer savory, fennel seeds, mustard seeds, cayenne pepper, cumin, turmeric, cinnamon, nutmeg, vanilla, cloves, ginger.

Salad and Side Dish Recipes

Vitamin Chicken Salad

Serves: 4
Prep time: 5 min

Ingredients:

3 cooked chicken breasts, shredded

1 yellow bell pepper, thinly sliced

1 red bell pepper, thinly sliced

1 small red onion, thinly sliced

1 small green apple, peeled and thinly sliced

1/2 cup toasted almonds, chopped

3 tbsp lemon juice

2 tbsp extra virgin olive oil

1 tbsp gluten-free mustard

salt and pepper, to taste

Directions:

In a deep salad bowl, combine the peppers, apple, chicken and almonds.

In a smaller bowl, whisk the mustard, olive oil, lemon juice, salt and pepper. Pour over the salad, toss to combine and serve.

Chicken, Lettuce and Avocado Salad

Serves: 4
Prep time: 5 min

Ingredients:

2 grilled chicken breasts, diced

1 avocado, peeled and diced

5-6 green lettuce leaves, cut in stripes

3-4 green onions, finely chopped

5-6 radishes, sliced

7-8 grape tomatoes, halved

3 tbsp lemon juice

3 tbsp extra virgin olive oil

1 tsp dried mint

salt and black pepper, to taste

Directions:

In a deep salad bowl, combine the avocados, lettuce, chicken, onions, radishes and grape tomatoes.

Season with mint, salt and pepper to taste.

Sprinkle with lemon juice and olive oil. Toss lightly and serve.

Tomato, Chicken and Arugula Salad

Serves: 4-5
Prep time: 10 min

Ingredients:

1 cup yellow cherry tomatoes, halved

1 cup cherry tomatoes, halved

1 cup cooked chicken, diced

½ small red onion, sliced and separated into rings

a bunch of arugula

1 cup baby spinach leaves

1 tbsp dried mint

2 tbsp extra virgin olive oil

1 tbsp balsamic vinegar

Directions:

In a salad bowl, combine the tomatoes, chicken, onion, spinach and arugula leaves.

In a cup, whisk the oil, vinegar and dried mint. Season with salt and pepper to taste, drizzle with the dressing, toss to combine, and serve.

Mashed Avocado and Chicken Salad

Serves: 4
Prep time: 5 min

Ingredients:

2 cooked chicken breasts, diced

1 small red onion, finely chopped

2 ripe avocados, mashed with a fork

3 tbsp lemon juice

1 tbsp extra virgin olive oil

1 tbsp fresh tarragon leaves, finely cut

salt and pepper, to taste

Directions:

Place the chicken in a medium sized salad bowl.

In a plate, mash the avocados using either a fork or a potato masher and add them to the chicken.

Add in the onion, tarragon, lemon juice and olive oil. Season with salt and black pepper to taste, stir to combine, and serve.

Easy Chicken and Egg Salad

Serves: 4
Prep time: 5 min

Ingredients:

2 cups cooked chicken, chopped

2 hard boiled eggs, diced

a bunch of arugula leaves

1 large apple, diced

1/2 cup walnuts, roasted

2 tbsp lemon juice

2 tbsp extra virgin olive oil

salt and pepper, to taste

Directions:

Roast walnuts in a preheated to 450 F oven for 2-3 minutes or until toasted.

In a deep salad bowl, combine the chicken, apple, eggs and arugula.

In a smaller bowl, whisk lemon juice, olive oil, salt and black pepper.

Pour over the chicken mixture. Top with walnuts and serve.

Beef, Spinach and Avocado Salad

Serves 4-5
Prep time: 5 min

Ingredients:

8 oz quality roast beef, thinly sliced

1 avocado, peeled and sliced

1 red onion, sliced and separated into rings

2 tomatoes, thinly sliced

3 cups baby spinach

2 tbsp extra virgin olive oil

salt, to taste

for the dressing:

2 tbsp lemon juice

1 tbsp extra virgin olive oil

1 tbsp mustard

Directions:

Combine all dressing ingredients in a deep bowl and whisk until smooth.

Heat olive oil in a large skillet and gently sauté the onions and beef. Cook until the beef is heated through.

Toss together the beef, spinach, tomatoes and avocado in a large salad bowl. Season with salt, drizzle with the dressing, and serve.

Steak Salad with Arugula and Avocado

Serves 4
Prep time: 7-8 min

Ingredients:

1 lb boneless beef sirloin steak, 1 inch thick

1 avocado, peeled and sliced

3 cups arugula leaves

1 red onion, sliced and separated into rings

salt and black pepper, to taste

2 tbsp extra virgin olive oil

for the dressing:

2 garlic cloves, crushed

2 tbsp extra virgin olive oil

1 tbsp balsamic vinegar

1/2 tsp dried basil

salt and black pepper, to taste

Directions:

Prepare the dressing by whisking all ingredients in a bowl.

In a heavy skillet, heat olive oil. Season the steak with salt and black pepper, and cook for 3-4 minutes, each side, on medium heat.

Set aside on a cutting board and leave to cool.

Slice against the grain.

Toss the steak with arugula, onion and avocado. Season with salt and pepper, drizzle with dressing, and serve.

Mediterranean Beef Salad

Serves 4-5
Prep time: 5 min

Ingredients:

8 oz quality roast beef, thinly sliced

1 avocado, peeled and diced

2 tomatoes, diced

1 cucumber, peeled and diced

1 yellow pepper, sliced

2 carrots, shredded

1 cup black olives, pitted and halved

2-3 fresh basil leaves, torn

2-3 fresh oregano leaves

1 tbsp balsamic vinegar

4 tbsp extra virgin olive oil

salt and black pepper, to taste

Directions:

Combine the avocado and all vegetables in a large salad bowl. Add in basil and oregano leaves.

Season with salt and pepper, drizzle with balsamic vinegar and olive oil and toss to combine. Top with beef and serve.

Ground Beef Salad with Creamy Avocado Dressing

Serves 4-5
Prep time: 5 min

Ingredients:

1 green lettuce, cut in stripes

2-3 green onions, finely cut

1 garlic clove, crushed

½ cup black olives, pitted and halved

4-5 radishes, sliced

8 oz ground beef, cooked

2 tbsp extra virgin olive oil

1/2 tsp ground cumin

1/2 tsp dried oregano

1 tsp paprika

salt and pepper, to taste

for the dressing:

1 avocado, peeled and cut

1 tbsp extra virgin olive oil

4 tbsp lemon juice

2 garlic cloves, cut

1 tbsp water

1/2 tsp salt

Directions:

Blend the dressing ingredients until smooth.

Heat olive oil in a medium saucepan and gently cook the ground beef and seasonings. Place the lettuce, cooked beef and all other salad ingredients in a bowl. Toss well to combine. Drizzle with dressing and serve.

Warm Leek and Sweet Potato Salad

Serves 4-5
Prep time: 30 min

Ingredients:

1.5 lb sweet potato, unpeeled, cut into 1 inch pieces

4 small leeks, trimmed and cut into 1 inch slices

5-6 white mushrooms, halved

1 cup baby arugula leaves

2 tbsp extra virgin olive oil

for the dressing

4 tbsp lemon juice

1 tbsp gluten-free mustard

1 tbsp 100% pure maple syrup (unprocessed)

Directions:

Preheat oven to 350F. Line a baking tray with baking paper. Place the sweet potato, leeks and mushrooms on the baking tray.

Drizzle with olive oil and toss to coat. Roast for 20 minutes or until golden.

Combine lemon juice, maple syrup and mustard in a small bowl or cup. Place the vegetables, mushrooms and baby arugula in a salad bowl and toss to combine.

Top with the dressing mixture, toss again, and serve.

Beet Salad with Walnuts

Serves: 4
Prep time: 25 min

Ingredients:

3 medium beets, steamed and diced

1 red onion, sliced

1/2 cup walnuts, halved

1 tbsp lemon juice

2 tbsp olive oil

4-5 mint leaves

½ tsp salt

Directions:

Wash the beets, trim the stems, and steam them over boiling water until cooked through.

Dice the beets and place them in a salad bowl. Add in walnuts, onion, lemon juice and olive oil and toss to combine.

Chill, and serve sprinkled with fresh mint leaves.

Warm Beet and Lentil Salad

Serves: 5-6
Prep time: 10 min

Ingredients:

1 14 oz can brown lentils, drained, rinsed

1 14 oz can sliced pickled beets, drained

1 cup baby arugula leaves

1 small red onion, chopped

2 garlic cloves, crushed

1 tbsp extra virgin olive oil

for the dressing

3 tbsp extra virgin olive oil

1 tbsp red wine vinegar

1 tsp summer savory

salt and black pepper, to taste

Directions:

Heat one tablespoon of olive oil in a frying pan and gently sauté onion for 2-3 minutes or until softened.

Add in garlic, lentils and beets. Cook, stirring, for 2 minutes.

Whisk together remaining olive oil, vinegar, summer savory, salt and pepper. Add to the lentils and toss to coat. Add in baby arugula, toss gently to combine and serve.

Avocado, Black Bean and Red Pepper Salad

Serves: 4-5
Prep time: 6-7 min

Ingredients:

2 avocados, peeled and diced

1 can black beans, drained

2 red bell peppers, diced

1-2 green onions, finely chopped

1 garlic clove, minced

3 tbsp chopped fresh coriander

3 tbsp lemon juice

2 tbsp extra virgin olive oil

½ tsp cumin

Directions:

Place the avocados, beans, bell peppers, green onions, garlic, coriander and cumin in a salad bowl.

Sprinkle with lemon juice and olive oil, toss to combine and serve immediately.

Easy Artichoke and Bean Salad

Serves: 5-6
Prep time: 15 min

Ingredients:

1 14 oz can white beans, drained

2-3 large handfuls podded broad beans

3 marinated artichoke hearts, quartered

for the dressing:

2 tbsp extra virgin olive oil

1 tbsp lemon juice

1 tbsp apple cider vinegar

1 tbsp fresh mint, chopped

salt and pepper, to taste

Directions:

Cook the broad beans in boiling, unsalted water for 2-3 minutes or until tender. Drain and refresh under running cold water.

Combine with the white beans and quartered marinated artichoke hearts in a large salad bowl.

In a smaller bowl, whisk olive oil, lemon juice, vinegar and mint. Pour over the bean mixture. Season with salt and pepper and toss gently to combine.

Cabbage, Carrots and Turnip Salad

Serves: 4
Prep time: 15 min

Ingredients:

7 oz white cabbage, shredded

7 oz carrots, shredded

5 oz white turnips, shredded

1 tbsp sesame seeds

½ a bunch of dill

2 tbsp white vinegar

2 tbsp extra virgin olive oil

salt and black pepper, to taste

Directions:

Combine the first three ingredients in a large salad bowl.

Add in sesame seeds, salt, vinegar and olive oil. Stir and sprinkle with dill.

Set aside for 5 minutes, stir again and serve.

Roasted Vegetable Salad

Serves: 4-5
Prep time: 30 min

Ingredients:

3 tomatoes, halved

1 zucchini, quartered

1 fennel bulb, thinly sliced

2 small eggplants, ends trimmed, quartered

1 large red pepper, halved, deseeded, cut into strips

2 medium onions, quartered

1 tsp dried oregano

2 tbsp extra virgin olive oil

for the dressing

3 tbsp fresh lemon juice

2 garlic cloves, chopped

Directions:

Place the zucchini, eggplant, pepper, fennel, onions, tomatoes and olive oil on a lined baking sheet. Season with salt, pepper and oregano and roast in a 500F oven until golden, about 15 minutes.

Combine the lemon juice and garlic in a bowl. Taste and season with salt and pepper.

Divide the vegetables in 4-5 plates. Top with the dressing and serve.

Mediterranean Avocado Salad

Serves: 4
Prep time: 3 min

Ingredients:

2 avocados, peeled, halved and cut into cubes

2 cups cherry tomatoes, halved

½ red onion, thinly sliced

1 large cucumber, halved, sliced

½ cup green olives, pitted, halved

½ cup black olives, pitted, sliced

7-8 fresh basil leaves, torn

½ cup parsley leaves, finely cut

4 tbsp extra virgin olive oil

3 tbsp red wine vinegar

Directions:

Place all the vegetables, basil, and olives, in a large salad bowl. Gently toss to combine then sprinkle with vinegar and olive oil.

Season with salt and pepper and gently toss again. Sprinkle with parsley and serve.

Spinach and Asparagus Salad

Serves: 4-5
Prep time: 7 min

Ingredients:

1 bunch asparagus, woody ends trimmed, cut into 3 inch lengths

1 bag baby spinach

1 medium cucumber, peeled and sliced

for the dressing:

2 tbsp extra virgin olive oil

1 tbsp red wine vinegar

2 garlic cloves, crushed

salt and pepper, to taste

1 tbsp toasted sesame seeds, to serve

Directions:

Cook the asparagus in a medium saucepan of boiling water for 3 minutes or until bright green and tender crisp. Wash with running cold water and drain well.

Whisk the oil, vinegar and garlic in a small bowl until smooth. Season with salt and pepper to taste.

Combine the asparagus, spinach and cucumber in a large salad bowl. Drizzle with the dressing, toss to combine, sprinkle with sesame seeds and serve.

Pumpkin and Spinach Salad

Serves: 4-5
Prep time: 25 min

Ingredients:

3 cups pumpkin, deseeded, peeled and cut into wedges

1 bag baby spinach leaves

2 tbsp toasted pine nuts

1 tbsp dried cranberries

1 tbsp 100% pure maple syrup (unprocessed)

1 tbsp sesame seeds

3 tbsp extra virgin olive oil

2 tbsp lemon juice

1 tbsp gluten-free mustard

Directions:

Preheat oven to 350F. Line a baking tray with baking paper. Place the pumpkin in a large bowl, drizzle with two tablespoons of olive oil and honey. Season with salt and pepper to taste. Toss until the pumpkin pieces are well coated.

Arrange the pumpkin wedges in a single layer on the lined baking tray.

Bake, turning once, for 20 minutes or until golden. Remove from the oven, sprinkle evenly with sesame seeds and return to the oven.

Bake for 1-2 minutes or until the seeds are lightly toasted. Set aside for to cool.

Combine the lemon juice, remaining olive oil and mustard in a small bowl. Whisk until smooth. Season with salt and pepper.

Place the pumpkin, spinach, pine nuts and cranberries in a large salad bowl. Drizzle with the dressing, gently toss and serve.

Easy Chickpea Salad

Serves: 3-4
Prep time: 2-3 min

Ingredients:

1 15 oz can chickpeas, drained

1 medium red onion, finely cut

1 cucumber, peeled and diced

2 tomatoes, sliced

a bunch of radishes, sliced

½ cup fresh parsley, finely chopped

2 tbsp extra virgin olive oil

1 tbsp balsamic vinegar

salt, to taste

Directions:

In a salad bowl, toss together the chickpeas, onion, cucumber, tomatoes and radishes. Add in the balsamic vinegar, olive oil and salt and stir.

Serve sprinkled with parsley.

Chickpea and Avocado Salad

Serves: 3-4
Prep time: 2-3 min

Ingredients:

1 15 oz can chickpeas, drained, or 1/2 cup dried chickpeas, boiled and drained

1 avocado, peeled and sliced

1 small red onion, chopped

1 cucumber, peeled and diced

2 tomatoes, diced

½ cup fresh coriander, finely chopped

2 tbsp extra virgin olive oil

1 tbsp balsamic vinegar

salt, to taste

Directions:

In a salad bowl, toss together the chickpeas, onion, cucumber, tomatoes and coriander.

Add in the sliced avocado, balsamic vinegar, olive oil and salt. Gently toss to combine and serve.

Homemade Hummus

Serves: 5-6
Prep time: 5 min

Ingredients:

1 15 oz can chickpeas, drained

1/3 cup tahini paste

3 tbsp extra virgin olive oil

½ lemon, juiced

2-3 small garlic cloves, chopped

1-2 tsp cumin, or to taste

1 tsp salt

water from the chickpea can

extra virgin olive oil, parsley, paprika for serving

Directions:

Drain the chickpeas and keep the juice in a small cup. If possible, remove the skins from the chickpeas.

Place the chickpeas in the blender and pulse.

Add the tahini, lemon juice, garlic, olive oil, cumin and salt, and blend until smooth, gradually adding the chickpea water to the mix until the mixture is completely smooth.

To serve, top with olive oil, parsley, and sprinkle with paprika.

Chickpea and Avocado Hummus

Serves: 4
Prep time: 2-3 min

Ingredients:

1 15 oz can chickpeas, drained

1 medium avocado, chopped

2 tbsp tahini

1/4 cup lemon juice

1 garlic clove, crushed

2 tbsp finely cut parsley

1 tbsp extra virgin olive oil

½ tsp paprika

a pinch of cumin

Directions:

Heat oil in a small frying pan over medium-high heat. Add half the chickpeas and cook, stirring, for 3-4 minutes or until just golden. Remove from heat and set aside to cool.

Blend the remaining chickpeas with avocado, tahini, lemon juice, garlic and cumin until smooth. Season with salt and pepper, to taste, and spoon the avocado hummus into a serving bowl.

Top with chickpeas and sprinkle with paprika and parsley.

Soup Recipes

Mediterranean Chicken Soup

Serves: 4
Prep time: 35 min

Ingredients:

3 chicken breasts

1 carrot, chopped

1 small zucchini, peeled and chopped

1 celery rib, chopped

1 small onion, chopped

1 bay leaf

6 cups water

6-7 black olives, pitted and halved

1/2 tsp salt

black pepper, to taste

fresh parsley, to serve

lemon juice, to serve

Directions:

Place the chicken breasts, onion, carrot, celery and bay leaf in a deep soup pot.

Add in salt, black pepper and 6 cups of water. Stir well and bring to a boil. Add zucchini and olives and reduce heat. Simmer for 30 minutes.

Remove chicken from the pot and set aside to cool. Shred it and return it back to the pot. Serve with lemon juice and sprinkled with parsley.

Chicken and Butternut Squash Soup

Serves: 4
Prep time: 35 min

Ingredients:

3 boneless chicken thighs, diced

1/2 onion, chopped

6-7 white mushrooms, chopped

1 small zucchini, peeled and diced

1 cup butternut squash, diced

1 tbsp tomato paste

5 cups water

1/4 tsp cumin

1 tsp paprika

3 tbsp extra virgin olive oil

Directions:

In a deep soup pot, heat olive oil and gently sauté onion, stirring occasionally. Add chicken and cook for 2-3 minutes. Stir in cumin, paprika and butternut squash.

Dilute the tomato paste in a cup of water and add to the soup. Add in the remaining water and bring to a boil. Reduce heat and simmer for 15 minutes then add the zucchini and mushrooms.

Simmer until butternut squash is tender. Season with salt and black pepper to taste.

Chicken and Sweet Potato Soup

Serves: 4
Prep time: 35 min

Ingredients:

3 boneless chicken tights, chopped

1 small onion, chopped

3 garlic cloves

1 sweet potato, skinned and diced

1 large carrot, chopped

1 red bell pepper, chopped

1 celery rib, chopped

1 bay leaf

1 tsp salt

1/2 cup fresh parsley leaves, finely cut

black pepper, to taste

Directions:

Place the chicken, bay leaf, celery, carrot, onion, red pepper, sweet potato and salt into a pot with 4 cups of cold water.

Bring to the boil, reduce heat and simmer for 30 minutes.

Season with salt and pepper, add in parsley, simmer for 2-3 minutes and serve.

Creamy Chicken Soup

Serves: 4
Prep time: 35 min

Ingredients:

4 chicken breasts

1 carrot, chopped

1 cup zucchini, peeled and chopped

2 cups cauliflower, broken into florets

1 celery rib, chopped

1 small onion, chopped

4 cups water

1/2 tsp salt

black pepper, to taste

Directions:

Place the chicken breasts, onion, carrot, celery, cauliflower and zucchini in a deep soup pot. Add in salt, black pepper and 4 cups of water. Stir and bring to a boil.

Simmer for 30 minutes then remove chicken from the pot and let it cool slightly.

Blend the soup until completely smooth. Shred or dice the chicken meat, return it back to the pot, stir and serve.

Broccoli and Chicken Soup

Serves: 4
Prep time: 35 min

Ingredients:

4 boneless chicken thighs, diced

1 small carrot, chopped

1 broccoli head, broken into florets

1 garlic clove, chopped

1 small onion, chopped

4 cups water

3 tbsp extra virgin olive oil

1/2 tsp salt

black pepper, to taste

Directions:

In a deep soup pot, heat olive oil and gently sauté broccoli for 2-3 minutes, stirring occasionally. Add in the onion, carrot, and chicken and cook, stirring, for 2-3 minutes. Stir in salt, black pepper and water.

Bring to a boil. Simmer for 30 minutes then remove from heat and set aside to cool.

In a blender or food processor, blend soup until completely smooth. Serve and enjoy!

Beef and Vegetable Soup

Serves 4-5
Prep time: 60 min

Ingredients:

1 lb stewing beef

1 large onion, chopped

1 cup mushrooms, chopped

2 carrots, chopped

1 celery rib, chopped

1 turnip, peeled, cubed

1 cup coarsely chopped cabbage

5 cups home cooked beef broth

2 tbsp tomato paste

1/2 cup parsley, chopped

3 tbsp extra virgin olive oil

salt and black pepper, to taste

Directions:

In a soup pot, heat olive oil and brown the beef. Add in the onions, mushrooms, carrots, turnip and celery and sauté over medium high heat for 3-4 minutes.

Add broth and bring to the boil. Reduce heat and simmer, covered, for 60 minutes.

Stir in the tomato paste. Add in the cabbage, parsley and salt and pepper. Simmer for 10 minutes more and serve.

Ground Beef and Vegetable Minestrone

Serves 4-5
Prep time: 35 min

Ingredients:

2 slices bacon, chopped

1 lb ground beef

2 cloves garlic, finely chopped

1 onion, chopped

1 celery rib, chopped

1 carrot, chopped

1 sweet potato, peeled and cubed

1 bay leaf

1 tsp dried basil

1 can tomatoes, chopped

3 cups home cooked beef broth

Directions:

In a large saucepan, cook bacon and ground beef until well done. Add in carrots, garlic, onion and celery.

Cook until the onions are translucent. Stir in the bay leaf, basil, tomatoes, sweet potato and beef broth.

Bring to a boil then reduce heat and simmer for about 35 minutes.

Italian Meatball Soup

Serves 4-5
Prep time: 30 min

Ingredients:

1 lb ground beef

1 small onion, grated

1 onion, chopped

1 egg, lightly beaten

2 garlic cloves, crushed

1 cup baby spinach, coarsely chopped

4-5 fresh basil leaves, finely chopped

1 cup tomato sauce

3 cups home cooked beef broth

2 tbsp extra virgin olive oil

salt and black pepper, to taste

Directions:

Combine ground beef, onion, garlic and egg in a large bowl. Season with salt and pepper to taste. Mix well with hands and roll teaspoonfuls of the mixture into balls. Place meatballs on a large plate.

Heat olive oil into a large deep saucepan and sauté onion and garlic until transparent. Add in tomato sauce and broth and bring to a boil over high heat. Stir in the meatballs.

Reduce heat to medium-low and simmer, uncovered, for 20 minutes. Add in spinach, basil, salt, and pepper and simmer, uncovered, until spinach is wilted, about 1 minute.

Rich Meatball Soup

Serves 4-5
Prep time: 30 min

Ingredients:

1 lb ground beef

1/2 onion, chopped

1/2 onion, grated

2 garlic cloves, chopped

1/2 celery rib, chopped

1 tomato, diced

2 carrots, diced

1 green pepper, chopped

3 cups water

1 cup fresh parsley, finely cut

3 tbsp extra virgin olive oil

½ tsp black pepper

1 tsp salt

Directions:

Combine the ground beef with, grated onion, black pepper and salt in a large bowl. Mix with hands and roll teaspoonfuls of the mixture into balls.

Heat the olive oil into a deep soup pot and sauté the onion, garlic, carrots, celery and pepper until just fragrant. Add in parsley and simmer for 2 more minutes. Serve with lemon juice.

Celery, Apple and Carrot Soup

Serves: 4-5
Prep time: 20 min

Ingredients:

2 celery stalks, chopped

1 large apple, chopped

1/2 onion, chopped

2 carrots, chopped

1 garlic clove, minced

4 cups home cooked chicken broth

3-4 tbsp extra virgin olive oil

1 tsp paprika

1 tsp grated ginger

salt and black pepper, to taste

Directions:

Heat the olive oil in a deep soup pot over medium-high heat. Gently sauté the onion, garlic and carrots for 3-4 minutes, stirring. Add in paprika, ginger, celery, apple and broth.

Bring to the boil then reduce heat and simmer, covered, for 15 minutes. Blend the soup until smooth and return to pan.

Cook over medium-high heat until heated through. Season with salt and pepper to taste and serve.

Easy Vegetable Soup

Serves: 4-5
Prep time: 35 min

Ingredients:

2 leeks, white parts only, well rinsed and thinly sliced

1 carrot, chopped

1 cup Brussels sprouts, halved

1 small sweet potato, peeled and diced

1 garlic clove, chopped

1 red pepper, chopped

1 yellow pepper, chopped

1 cup white mushrooms, halved

4 cups water

3 tbsp extra virgin olive oil

salt and black pepper, to taste

Directions:

Heat the olive oil in a large soup pot. Add in the leeks and cook over low heat for 2-3 minutes.

Stir in the Brussels sprouts, carrot, garlic, peppers and sweet potato and cook for about 5 minutes, stirring. Add the water and the mushrooms and bring to a boil.

Reduce heat and simmer, uncovered, for 30 minutes, or until the vegetables are tender but still holding their shape. Season with salt and pepper to taste and serve.

Curried Parsnip Soup

Serves: 4-5
Prep time: 40 min

Ingredients:

1.5 lb parsnips, peeled, chopped

1 onion, chopped

2 garlic cloves, chopped

2 tbsp extra virgin olive oil

1 tbs curry powder

4 cups water

1/2 cup coconut milk

salt and black pepper, to taste

Directions:

In a deep saucepan, gently sauté the onion and garlic together with the curry powder. Add in the parsnips and sauté, stirring often, for 5-6 minutes.

Add 4 cups of water, bring to a boil, and simmer for 30 minutes or until the parsnips are tender.

Set aside to cool then blend in batches until smooth. Return soup to the pan, stir in the coconut milk and heat through. Season with salt and pepper to taste.

Mushroom and Kale Soup

Serves: 4-5
Prep time: 30 min

Ingredients:

1 onion, chopped

1 carrot, chopped

1 zucchini, peeled and diced

10 white mushrooms, chopped

1 bunch kale (10 oz), stemmed and coarsely chopped

3 cups home cooked chicken broth or water

4 tbsp extra virgin olive oil

salt and black pepper. to taste

Directions:

Gently heat the olive oil in a large soup pot. Add in the onions, carrot and mushrooms and cook until the vegetables are tender.

Stir in the zucchini, kale and chicken broth. Season to taste with salt and pepper and simmer for 20 minutes.

Spinach Soup

Serves: 4-5
Prep time: 35 min

Ingredients:

14 oz frozen spinach, slightly thawed

1 large onion, chopped

1 small carrot, chopped

1 small zucchini, peeled and chopped

3 cups hot water

4 tbsp extra virgin olive oil

1 tbsp paprika

salt and black pepper, to taste

salt, to taste

Directions:

Heat the oil in a deep cooking pot. Add in the onion and carrot and cook for 3-4 minutes, until tender. Add in paprika, spinach, zucchini and water and stir.

Season with salt and black pepper and bring to the boil. Reduce heat and simmer for around 30 minutes.

Mediterranean Lentil Soup

Serves: 4-5
Prep time: 20 min

Ingredients:

1 cup red lentils

2 carrots, chopped

1 onion, chopped

1 garlic clove, chopped

1 small red pepper, chopped

1 can tomatoes, chopped

½ can chickpeas, drained

½ can white beans, drained

1 celery stalk, chopped

1 tbsp paprika

1 tsp ginger, grated

1 tsp ground cumin

3 tbsp extra virgin olive oil

Directions:

Heat the olive oil in a deep soup pot and gently sauté the onions, garlic, red pepper and ginger. Add in 5 cups of water, lentils, chickpeas, white beans, tomatoes, carrots, celery, and cumin.

Bring to a boil then lower heat and simmer for 20 minutes, or until the lentils are tender.

Purée half the soup in a food processor. Return the puréed soup to the pot, stir and serve.

Carrot and Chickpea Soup

Serves: 4-5
Prep time: 20 min

Ingredients:

4 carrots, chopped

1 onion, chopped

1 garlic clove, crushed

4 cups vegetable broth

1 can chickpeas, undrained

½ cup orange juice

3-4 tbsp extra virgin olive oil

1 tsp paprika

½ tsp ginger

salt and black pepper, to taste

Directions:

Heat the olive oil in a deep soup pot over medium-high heat. Gently sauté the onion, garlic and carrots for 3-4 minutes, stirring.

Add in paprika, ginger, orange juice, broth and chickpeas.

Bring to the boil then reduce heat and simmer, covered, for 10 minutes.

Blend the soup until smooth and return to pan. Cook over medium-high heat until heated through. Season with salt and pepper to taste and serve.

Minted Pea Soup

Serves: 4
Prep time: 10 min

Ingredients:

1 onion, chopped

3-4 garlic cloves, chopped

4 cups vegetable broth

2 tbsp dried mint leaves

1 16 oz bag frozen green peas

3 tbsp extra virgin olive oil

fresh mint, finely chopped, to serve

Directions:

Heat the oil in a large saucepan over medium-high heat and sauté the onion and garlic for 3-4 minutes.

Add in the dried mint, peas and vegetable broth and bring to the boil. Cover, reduce heat, and simmer for 10 minutes.

Remove from heat and set aside to cool slightly, then blend in batches, until smooth.

Return the soup to the saucepan over medium-low heat and cook until heated through. Season with salt and pepper. Serve sprinkled with fresh mint.

Main Dish Recipes

Walnut Pesto Stuffed Chicken

Serves: 4
Prep time: 35 min

Ingredients:

4 large chicken breasts

for the walnut pesto

1/2 cup walnuts, chopped

10 fresh basil leaves

1 garlic clove

1 tbsp chia seeds

2-3 green olives

4 tbsp extra virgin olive oil

1 tbsp lemon juice

salt and black pepper, to taste

Directions:

In a food processor, blend together the walnuts, olives, basil, olive oil, garlic, chia seeds and lemon juice until completely smooth.

Carefully butterfly each chicken breast. Cover with plastic wrap and beat with a heavy object until the breast is flattened.

Put a tablespoon of the walnut mixture in each breast and roll over the top part like a flap. Season with salt and black pepper and bake at 375F for 35 minutes.

Chicken with Olive Paste

Serves: 4
Prep time: 40 min

Ingredients:

2 chicken breasts (each cut into 2 cutlets)

2 garlic cloves, crushed

for the olive paste:

2 tbsp olive oil

2 cloves garlic, peeled

2/3 cup pitted black olives

2 tbsp capers

1 tbsp tomato paste

1 tbsp basil, chopped

3 tbsp extra virgin olive oil

salt and pepper, to taste

Directions:

Place the garlic cloves into a food processor together with the olives, capers, basil, tomato paste and olive oil. Blend until smooth. Season to taste with salt and pepper.

Gently heat oil in a skillet on medium heat. Add in the chicken cutlets and cook each side for 4-5 minutes.

Serve each cutlet topped with olive paste.

Mediterranean Chicken Stew

Serves: 4
Prep time: 35 min

Ingredients:

4 chicken breasts

1 onion, chopped

1 small zucchini, peeled and chopped

1 red bell pepper, chopped

1 cup tomato sauce

1 cup assorted olives, pitted

1 tsp dried basil

1/2 cup fresh parsley, finely chopped

3 tbsp extra virgin olive oil

Directions:

In a deep pan, heat olive oil and seal the chicken breasts. Set aside in a plate.

In the same pan, gently sauté the onion and bell pepper, stirring, for 2-3 minutes, or until the onion has softened. Return the chicken to the pan. Add in zucchini, tomato sauce, olives, basil, salt and pepper.

Cover the pan and bring to a boil. Reduce heat and simmer for 30 minutes, or until the chicken is cooked through. Sprinkle with fresh parsley and serve.

Chicken Drumstick Casserole

Serves: 4
Prep time: 35 min

Ingredients:

8 chicken drumsticks

1 head broccoli, cut into florets

1 leek, sliced

1 garlic clove, crushed

1 sweet potato, peeled and cubed

1 carrot, cut

1 tsp dried rosemary

4 tbsp olive oil

1 tsp dried oregano

salt and black pepper, to taste

Directions:

Heat the olive oil in a non stick frying pan over medium heat. Add the chicken drumsticks and cook, turning occasionally, for 3-4 minutes, or until sealed.

Transfer the chicken to a casserole and add in the vegetables. Sprinkle with salt, pepper and oregano and bake in a preheated to 375F oven until cooked through.

Hunter Style Chicken

Serves: 4-5
Prep time: 45 min

Ingredients:

1 chicken (3-4 lbs), cut into pieces

1 onions, sliced

2 red peppers, sliced

6-7 white button mushrooms, sliced

1 can tomatoes, diced and drained

3 garlic cloves, thinly sliced

2 tbsp extra virgin olive oil

salt and black pepper, to taste

1/2 cup parsley leaves, finely cut

Directions:

Heat the olive oil in a deep pan on medium heat. Working in batches, brown the chicken pieces, for 5-6 minutes each side. Add in the onions, garlic and peppers together with the mushrooms and canned tomatoes.

Lower the heat and cover the pan with the lid slightly ajar.

Let the chicken simmer for about 40 minutes, turning from time to time. Sprinkle with parsley, set aside to rest a few minutes before serving to keep the juices inside and serve.

Healthy Chicken Meatballs

Serves: 4-5
Prep time: 30 min

Ingredients:

2 lbs ground chicken meat

1 onion, very finely cut

2 eggs, lightly whisked

1 tbsp chia seeds

1 tbsp parsley, finely chopped

1 tbs ground ginger

1/2 tsp cumin

2 tbsp extra virgin olive oil

1 cup home cooked chicken broth or water

1 can tomatoes, drained and diced

1 tbsp tomato paste

tsp sugar

Directions:

Preheat the oven to 350F. Line a baking tray with baking paper.

Combine the ground chicken, onion, eggs, chia seeds, parsley, ginger, salt and cumin in a bowl. Using your hands, mix everything until it is combined well.

Roll the chicken mixture into walnut sized meatballs and arrange them on the baking tray. Bake for 10 minutes until light golden.

In a deep frying pan, heat olive oil on medium heat. Stir in the remaining ginger. Add in tomatoes, sugar and stir.

Add chicken broth and tomato paste, and bring to a boil, then reduce heat and simmer for 5 minutes. Add the meatballs and simmer for 20 more minutes or until the meat is cooked through and the sauce has thickened.

Bacon Wrapped Chicken Breasts

Serves: 4
Prep time: 45 min

Ingredients:

2 large boneless chicken breasts

10 slices sugar-free bacon

3-4 canned artichoke hearts, chopped

3-4 sun-dried tomatoes, finely chopped

2 garlic cloves, crushed

a few fresh rosemary leaves, chopped

Mix the artichoke hearts and the sun-dried tomatoes in a small bowl.

Directions:

Preheat the oven to 375F. Carefully butterfly each chicken breast ensuring not to slice all the way through.

Season with salt and spoon ¼ of the stuffing in the middle of each breast. Spread it as evenly as possible and roll the breasts tightly.

Wrap two slices of bacon around each chicken breast and secure the bacon with a toothpick.

Arrange the chicken rolls in a baking dish, cover with a lid or aluminum foil and bake at 375F for 35 minutes. Remove foil and return to the oven for 10 minutes or until bacon is crispy.

Healthy Chicken Dippers

Serves: 4
Prep time: 20 min

Ingredients:

1 pound boneless, skinless chicken breast, cut into thin strips

2 egg, whisked

1/2 cup shredded coconut

1/4 cup almond flour

1 tbsp sesame seeds

1 tsp garlic powder

1/3 tsp salt

2 tbsp extra virgin olive oil

Directions:

Preheat the oven to 350F. Whisk the eggs in a small bowl. In another bowl, mix the coconut, almond flour, sesame seeds, garlic powder and salt. Dip each chicken strip in the whisked eggs, then in the coconut mixture. Coat on all sides and set aside on a plate.

Place a large skillet over medium heat. Add olive oil and when it is hot add in some of the strips. Cook for about two minutes then flip each chicken strip and cook on the other side. Set aside to cool and serve.

Spicy Mustard Chicken

Serves: 4
Prep time: 65 min

Ingredients:

4 chicken breasts

2 garlic cloves, crushed

1/2 cup home cooked chicken broth or water

3 tbsp gluten-free mustard

2 tbsp extra virgin olive oil

1 tsp chili powder

Directions:

In a small bowl, mix the mustard, olive oil, chicken broth, garlic and chili. Marinate the chicken for 30 minutes.

Bake at 375F for 35 minutes.

Garlic Chicken

Serves: 4
Prep time: 35 min

Ingredients:

4 boneless skinless chicken breasts

5 garlic cloves, crushed

3 lemon slices

6-7 green olives, pitted

1 tbsp dried rosemary

2 tbsp extra virgin olive oil

salt and pepper, to taste

Directions:

Gently heat the olive oil in a skillet over medium-low heat and sauté the garlic for about a minute, stirring.

Add the lemon slices to the bottom of the pan. Lay the chicken breasts on top of the lemon. Add in the rosemary and the olives.

Season with salt and pepper to taste, cover the pan, and cook, on medium-low, for 20 minutes or until the chicken breasts are cooked through, turning once.

Uncover and cook for 2-3 minutes, until the liquid evaporates.

Chicken Puttanesca

Serves: 4
Prep time: 30 min

Ingredients:

4 boneless chicken breasts

2 tbsp extra virgin olive oil

for the sauce:

2 tbsp extra virgin olive oil

4 garlic cloves, crushed

1 small onion, diced

1/2 cup green olives, pitted and chopped

2 tbsp capers, drained and coarsely chopped

3 boneless anchovy fillets, coarsely chopped

2 tomatoes, diced

1 tbsp tomato paste

1/2 tsp paprika

salt and black pepper, to taste

Directions:

Heat two tablespoons of olive oil in a large skillet and brown the chicken for about 2 minutes, each side. Cover with a lid and cook for about 10-15 minutes, or until cooked through. Set aside on 4 plates.

In the same skillet, heat two tablespoons of olive oil. Add in garlic, onions, anchovies, olives, capers and paprika. Gently sauté these ingredients, stirring constantly, for about one minute.

Add in the tomatoes and tomato paste, season with salt and

pepper and cook over high heat for 5-6 minutes or until the tomatoes are cooked and the sauce thickens. Divide the sauce between the chicken breasts and serve.

Grilled Chicken with Herbs

Serves: 4
Prep time: 50 min

Ingredients:

8 chicken thigh or 4 chicken breasts

½ cup parsley leaves

¼ cup oregano leaves

¼ cup cilantro leaves

3 garlic cloves, crushed

2 tbsp extra virgin olive oil

½ tsp salt

1/2 tsp turmeric

Directions:

Place the garlic, herbs, olive oil, salt, paprika and turmeric in a food processor or blender and pulse until smooth. Pour this mixture over the chicken and stir to coat meat well. Refrigerate for at least 20 minutes.

Arrange the chicken on a baking tray and bake for 30 minutes or until cooked through.

Greek Style Chicken Skewers

Serves: 4
Prep time: 50 min

Ingredients:

2 lbs chicken breasts, diced

4 small zucchinis, diced

3 tbsp extra virgin olive oil

1 lemon, juiced

2 garlic cloves, crushed

1 tsp dried oregano

1 tsp dried rosemary

12 wooden skewers

Directions:

Thread chicken and zucchini alternately onto each of 12 skewers. Place in a shallow dish. Combine extra virgin olive oil and lemon juice, garlic and oregano. Pour over chicken. Turn to coat. Marinate for at least 30 minutes.

Preheat a barbecue plate on medium-high heat. Cook skewers for 4 minutes each side or until chicken is just cooked through.

Chicken and Chickpea Casserole

Serves: 4
Prep time: 40 min

Ingredients:

8 chicken drumsticks

2 leeks, trimmed, thinly sliced

1 garlic clove, crushed

1 can chickpeas, drained and rinsed (Note: Opt for BPA-free cans)

3 ripe tomatoes, diced

1 tsp dried rosemary

3 tbsp extra virgin olive oil

cooked quinoa, to serve

Directions:

In a casserole, gently heat the oil over medium-high heat. Brown the chicken tights for 1-2 minutes, each side.

Add in the leeks and garlic and cook, stirring, for 2 minutes or until soft. Add in the tomatoes, chickpeas, and rosemary and bring to a boil.

Cover and simmer for 35 minutes or until the chicken is tender. Season with salt and pepper and serve with quinoa.

Greek Chicken Casserole

Serves: 4
Prep time: 45 min

Ingredients:

8 chicken tights

1 onion, chopped

4-5 potatoes, peeled and cubed

1 carrot, chopped

1 lb green beans, trimmed and chopped

1 cup diced, tomatoes

2 garlic cloves, chopped

3 tbsp extra virgin olive oil

salt and black pepper, to taste

Directions:

Heat oil in a large casserole dish over medium heat. Add in onion and chicken and cook for a minute, stirring. Add in black pepper, carrot and garlic and sauté for another minute. Add potatoes and cook for 2 minutes, or until they begin to brown. Stir in beans and tomatoes.

Sprinkle with salt and black pepper to taste. Cover, and bake for 40 minutes, stirring halfway through.

Chicken and Lentil Stew

Serves: 4-5
Prep time: 35 min

Ingredients:

4 chicken breasts, diced

1/2 cup red lentils, rinsed

1 carrot, chopped

1 small onion, chopped

1 garlic clove, chopped

1 celery stalk, chopped

1 small red pepper, chopped

1 can tomatoes, chopped

1 tbsp paprika

1 tsp ginger, grated

3 tbsp extra virgin olive oil

1/2 cup fresh parsley leaves, finely cut, to serve

Directions:

Heat olive oil in a casserole and gently brown the chicken, stirring. Add in onions, garlic, celery, carrot, pepper, paprika and ginger. Cook, stirring constantly, for 2-3 minutes.

Add in the lentils and tomatoes and bring to a boil. Lower heat, cover, and simmer for 30 minutes, or until the lentils are tender and the chicken is cooked through.

Serve sprinkled with fresh parsley.

Chicken with Mustard Lentils and Spinach

Serves: 4-5
Prep time: 35 min

Ingredients:

2 chicken breasts, diced

1 cup green lentils, rinsed

1 carrot, chopped

5-6 green onions, finely cut

2 garlic cloves, chopped

1 celery stalk, chopped

5-6 white button mushrooms, cut

1 cup fresh spinach, chopped

2 cups vegetable broth

2 tbsp gluten-free mustard

1 tbsp paprika

3 tbsp extra virgin olive oil

Directions:

Heat the olive oil in a casserole and gently brown the chicken, stirring. Add in onions, garlic, celery, carrot, mushrooms and paprika and cook, stirring constantly, for 2-3 minutes.

Add in the lentils and broth and bring to a boil. Lower heat, cover, and simmer for 30 minutes, or until the lentils are tender and the chicken is cooked through.

Stir in the mustard and spinach and cook for 3-4 minutes more.

Stephanie's Meatloaf

Serves: 4-5
Prep time: 60 min

Ingredients:

2 lbs ground beef

1 small onion, very finely cut

2 eggs, lightly beaten

1/3 cup almond meal

1/2 cup fresh parsley, finely cut

2 tbsp tomato paste

3 hard boiled eggs, halved

3 pickled gherkins, quartered

2 carrots, quartered

4 tbsp extra virgin olive oil

1 tsp garlic powder

1/2 tsp black pepper, salt, to taste

Directions:

Place the ground beef, onion, eggs, almond meal, tomato paste, parsley, salt, garlic powder and black pepper in a bowl and combine well with hands.

Take one half of the beef mixture and place into a loaf pan. Press down until well packed and make a slight well in the center. Place the eggs, gherkins and carrots in the well and cover with remaining ground meat mixture. Press down well.

Sprinkle with olive oil and bake in a preheated to 350F oven for 40 minutes.

Spicy Burgers and Vegetables

Serves: 4
Prep time: 20 min

Ingredients:

1.25 lb ground beef

1 tsp salt

1 tsp black pepper

1/2 tsp cumin

1 tbsp tomato puree

1 tsp smoked paprika

1 tsp garlic powder

1 tbsp dried parsley

2 red bell peppers, cut into thin strips

1 small onion, sliced

3-4 mushrooms, sliced

2 tomatoes, sliced

1 avocado, sliced

4 lettuce leaves, to serve

Directions:

Place ground beef in a bowl, add in tomato puree and all seasonings. Mix with hands and form 4 patties. Set them on a plate and sprinkle with a little olive oil.

In a skillet, gently sauté sliced mushrooms, peppers and onion for 4-5 minutes, stirring.

Grill burgers over medium heat for 4-5 minutes each side for medium cooked.

Serve burgers on a piece of lettuce with a tomato slice, 2 avocado slices and the sautéed peppers, onion and mushrooms.

Ground Beef and Brussels Sprouts

Serves: 4
Prep time: 20 min

Ingredients:

6 oz ground beef

1/2 onion, finely cut

2 garlic cloves, crushed

½ cup grated sweet potato

1 cup grated Brussels sprouts

1 egg, boiled

1 tbsp extra virgin olive oil

Directions:

In a medium saucepan, heat the olive oil over medium heat. Gently sauté the onion and garlic until the onion is soft and translucent. Add in the beef and the sweet potato and cook until the meat is fully cooked.

Stir in the Brussels sprouts and cook for about 5 minutes more. Season with salt and pepper to taste and serve topped with a boiled egg.

Roast Beef with Quince, Parsnips and Carrots

Serves 6
Prep time: 60-70 min

Ingredients:

2-3 lb roast beef round

4 parsnips, peeled, quartered lengthwise

6 carrots, quartered lengthwise

2 quinces, peeled, cored and cubed

1 cup home cooked beef or chicken broth

2 tbsp apple puree

1 tbsp gluten-free mustard

3 tbsp extra virgin olive oil

black pepper, to taste

Directions:

Whisk together beef broth, apple puree and mustard until smooth.

Heat the olive oil in a large frying pan over high heat and seal all sides of the roast. Transfer roast to a baking dish.

Arrange the parsnips around the beef. Sprinkle with black pepper and roast for 15 minutes. Add in the carrots and roast, stirring the vegetables once, for a further 25 minutes.

Add in the quince. Brush the beef with the apple puree and mustard mixture.

Cover and bake at 325F 30 minutes, or until cooked to your liking.

Eggplant With Ground Beef

Serves: 6
Prep time: 45 min

Ingredients:

1 lb ground beef

2 eggplants, peeled and cut into thick rounds

1 tbsp salt

1 onion, chopped

2 garlic cloves, crushed

1/2 tsp ground cinnamon

1/2 tsp ground nutmeg

1/4 tsp ground coriander

1 can tomatoes, undrained, chopped

1/2 cup parsley leaves, finely chopped

2 eggs

3 tbsp coconut milk

4 tbsp extra virgin olive oil

salt and black pepper, to taste

Directions:

Peel and cut the eggplant and place the slices on a plate. Sprinkle with a tablespoon of salt and set aside for 30 minutes, then rinse and pat dry.

Heat olive oil in a deep frying pan over medium-high heat. Fry the eggplant slices in batches for 2-3 minutes each side or until golden. Set aside in a plate.

In the same pan, sauté onion and garlic for 2-3 minutes or until transparent. Add in ground beef and spice, mix well and sauté until it turns light brown. Add in tomatoes and parsley and simmer until the tomato sauce thickens.

Place half the eggplant slices in an ovenproof baking dish. Cover with beef and tomato mixture and top with remaining eggplant.

Whisk two eggs with coconut milk. Pour over the meat and eggplant mixture.

Bake for 30 minutes or until golden. Set aside for five minutes and serve.

Steak with Olives and Mushrooms

Serves: 6
Prep time: 20 min

Ingredients:

1 lb boneless beef sirloin steak, 3/4-inch thick, cut into 4 pieces

1 large onion, sliced

5-6 white mushrooms

1/2 cup green olives, coarsely chopped

4 tbsp extra virgin olive oil

1 cup parsley leaves, finely cut

Directions:

Heat olive oil in a heavy bottomed skillet over medium-high heat. Cook the steaks until well browned on both sides then set aside in a plate.

Gently sauté the onion in the same skillet, for 2-3 minutes, stirring occasionally. Add in the mushrooms and olives and cook until the mushrooms are done.

Return the steaks to the skillet, cover, and cook for 5-6 minutes. Stir in parsley and serve.

Mediterranean Beef Casserole

Serves: 5-6
Prep time: 35 min

Ingredients:

2 lbs boneless lean beef stew meat, cut into 1 1/2-inch cubes

1 onion, sliced

2 garlic cloves, chopped

2 carrots, cut

1 fennel bulb, trimmed and thinly sliced vertically

1 zucchini, cut

3 tomatoes, quartered

2 tbsp tomato paste

1/2 cup black olives, pitted

1/2 cup home cooked chicken broth

2 tbsp extra virgin olive oil

1 bay leaf

1 tsp dried basil

salt and black pepper, to taste

Directions:

Heat the olive oil in a deep saucepan and brown the beef. Dilute the tomato paste in the broth and pour over the beef mixture.

Add in the olives, bay leaf and basil and simmer, covered, for 60 minutes. Add all vegetables and simmer for 20 minutes more.

Beef with Melting Onions

Serves: 6
Prep time: 120 min

Ingredients:

2 lb stewing beef

4 large onions, sliced

3 garlic cloves, chopped

1 bay leaf

1/2 cup home cooked chicken broth

4 tbsp extra virgin olive oil

1 tsp cinnamon

1/2 tsp ginger powder

salt and black pepper, to taste

Directions:

Heat olive oil in a large saucepan and brown the beef. Add in onions and garlic and sauté for 2-3 minutes, stirring. Add cinnamon, ginger, bay leaf, black pepper and chicken broth.

Bring to a boil. Reduce heat to low, cover, and simmer for 2 hours, stirring occasionally, until the beef is tender.

Beef with Mushrooms

Serves: 4-5
Prep time: 90 min

Ingredients:

2 lb stewing beef

2 lb white mushrooms, sliced

1 onion, finely cut

6 tbsp extra virgin olive oil

1/2 cup white wine

1 tsp dried thyme

1 tsp salt

1/2 cup fresh parsley, finely cut

black pepper, to taste

Directions:

Gently heat olive oil in a deep saucepan and cook the beef until well browned. Add in onion and sauté for 1-2 minutes until fragrant. Add in thyme and black pepper and stir to combine.

Add the mushrooms and the white wine, cover, and simmer, stirring from time to time, for 90 minutes or until the beef is cooked through.

Lamb Asparagus Stew

Serves 4
Prep time: 30-40 min

Ingredients:

1 lb cubed lamb

2 lbs fresh asparagus, trimmed and cut into 2 inch pieces

1 lb shallots

1 cup water

juice of 1 lemon

1 tsp dry mint

1 tsp dry oregano

salt and black pepper, to taste

3 tbsp extra virgin olive oil

Directions:

Wash and trim asparagus. Cut into 2 inch pieces.

Heat olive oil in a deep casserole and brown lamb pieces on moderate heat. Add in shallots and cook for a few minutes.

Add water and herbs, cover, and cook for an hour or until the meat is tender.

Stir in asparagus. Season with salt and black pepper to taste and cook for 6-7 minutes more. Add lemon juice and serve.

Spring Lamb Stew

Serves 4
Prep time: 30-40 min

Ingredients:

1 lb lamb cubed lamb

1 lb white mushrooms, chopped

4 cups fresh spring onions, chopped

1 tomato, chopped

3 tbsp extra virgin olive oil

1 tbsp paprika

1 cup fresh mint, finely cut

3 cups fresh parsley, finely cut

Directions:

Heat olive oil in a deep casserole. Gently brown lamb pieces for 2-3 minutes. Add in mushrooms and cook for a minute more, stirring.

Stir in paprika, cover, and cook for an hour or until tender. Add in spring onions, tomatoes, mint and parsley and simmer for 10 minutes more.

Uncover and cook until almost all the liquid evaporates.

Pork Skewers

Serves: 6
Prep time: 30-40 min

Ingredients:

6 pork loin medallions, cut into cubes

4 large onions, quartered

2 green peppers, deseeded, cut into 2 inch pieces

1 large zucchini, cubed

30 white mushrooms, whole

12 wooden skewers

Directions:

Thread pork cubes onto skewers, dividing them with mushrooms, zucchini, peppers and onions.

Preheat BBQ grill to medium heat. Grill the skewers for about 5-6 minutes each side for medium cooked.

Transfer to a plate, cover with foil, and set aside for 5 minutes to rest.

Salmon Kebabs

Serves: 4-5
Prep time: 30 min

Ingredients:

2 shallots, ends trimmed, halved

2 zucchinis, cut in 2 inch cubes

1 cup cherry tomatoes

6 skinless salmon fillets, cut into 1 inch pieces

3 limes, cut into thin wedges

Directions:

Preheat the barbecue or char grill on medium-high. Thread fish cubes onto skewers, then zucchinis, shallots and tomatoes. Repeat to make 12 kebabs. Bake the kebabs for about 3 minutes each side for medium cooked.

Transfer to a plate, cover with foil and set aside for 5 minutes to rest.

Mediterranean Baked Salmon

Serves: 4-5
Prep time: 35 min

Ingredients:

2 (6 oz) boneless salmon fillets

1 tomato, thinly sliced

1 onion, thinly sliced

1 tbsp capers

3 tbsp olive oil

1 tsp dried oregano

salt and black pepper, to taste

Directions:

Preheat oven to 350F. Place the salmon fillets in a baking dish, sprinkle with oregano, top with onion and tomato slices, drizzle with olive oil, and sprinkle with capers.

Cover the dish with foil and bake for 30 minutes, or until the fish flakes easily.

Almond and Oregano Crusted Fish Fillets

Serves: 4
Prep time: 10 min

Ingredients:

4 white fish fillets

1 tsp dried oregano

1/2 cup raw almonds, chopped

1 garlic clove, chopped

3 egg whites, beaten

salt and pepper, to taste

Directions:

Blend the garlic, oregano and almonds in a food processor until a light crumb is formed. Stir in salt and black pepper and place on a plate.

Whisk egg whites in a deep bowl. Dip each fish fillet in the beaten egg whites then roll it in the almond mixture.

Place coated fish on a lined baking tray and bake at 375F for 6-7 minutes each side.

Easy Coconut Fish Curry

Serves: 4
Prep time: 10 min

Ingredients:

4 skinless, boneless white fish fillets, cut into chunks

1 cup basmati rice

1 large onion, chopped

2 garlic cloves, chopped

1 can tomatoes, diced

1 zucchini, peeled and diced

3 tbsp curry paste

1 can coconut milk

1 tbsp extra virgin olive oil

1 tsp coriander, roughly chopped

Cook the rice following package directions.

Directions:

Heat the oil in a large saucepan over medium heat and saute the onion for 5-10 minutes until softened and starting to color. Add the garlic and tomatoes and cook for 2 min more. Add the curry paste, stir well and pour in the coconut milk. Bring to a boil.

Stir in the fish and zucchini and simmer gently for 5-7 minutes until just cooked through.

Serve over rice and sprinkled with coriander.

Lamb Tagine with Green Olives and Lemon

Serves 4
Prep time: 30-40 min

Ingredients:

3 lb boneless lamb shoulder, cut into 1-inch pieces

4-5 large carrots, thinly sliced

1 onion, chopped

2 garlic cloves, crushed

2 cups green olives, pitted

3 cups water

3 tbsp extra virgin olive oil

1 tbsp lemon zest

1 tbsp paprika

1 tsp cumin

1 tsp ground coriander

1 tsp cinnamon

a pinch of saffron threads, crumbled

1 tsp black pepper

1 tsp salt

3 tbsp lemon juice

1 cup cilantro leaves, chopped

1/2 cup fresh mint, finely cut

Directions:

In a large bowl, mix the olive oil, garlic, lemon zest, paprika, coriander, cumin, black pepper, saffron, cinnamon and salt. Add the lamb and toss to coat. Refrigerate for at least 4 hours.

Place the lamb and spices into a tagine or a casserole. Add the water, carrots and onion and bring to a boil.

Cover and simmer over low heat until the lamb is tender, about 2 hours.

Stir in the olives and cook for 2 minutes. Stir in the mint, cilantro and lemon juice and serve.

Beef Tagine with Sweet Potatoes

Serves: 4-5
Prep time: 120 min

Ingredients:

2 lbs stewing beef

1 onion, finely chopped

1/2 cup water

1 bunch of fresh cilantro

1 bunch of fresh parsley

2 ripe tomatoes, peeled and sliced

1 lb sweet potatoes, peeled and cut into slices

4-5 tbsp extra virgin olive oil

½ tsp turmeric

½ tsp black pepper

1/2 tsp paprika

1/4 tsp ground ginger

½ tsp cumin

Directions:

In an deep casserole dish, heat olive oil and saute the beef until well browned. Add in onion, water, turmeric, salt, black pepper and all remaining spices.

Tie the parsley and cilantro together into a bouquet and place on top of the beef. Cover, bring to a boil, immediately reduce heat, and simmer for 60 minutes until the meat is tender.

Remove from heat, remove the parsley and cilantro bouquet and add the sweet potatoes on top of the beef. Place the tomatoes on top of the sweet potatoes. Cover again and simmer for 40 minutes, until the meat and potatoes are tender.

Ground Beef and Cabbage Casserole

Serves: 4-5
Prep time: 50 min

Ingredients:

1 lb ground beef

1/2 cabbage, shredded

1/2 onion, chopped

2 leeks, white part only, chopped

1 tomato, diced

1 tbsp paprika

1/2 tsp cumin

½ tsp black pepper

4 tbsp extra virgin olive oil

salt, to taste

Directions:

In a deep saucepan, sauté the onion and leeks in olive oil until tender. Add in the ground beef, tomato, paprika, cumin, salt and black pepper.

Place the shredded cabbage on the bottom of an ovenproof baking dish. Cover with the beef mixture. Cover with a lid or aluminum foil and bake at 325F for 40 minutes.

Ground Beef and Lentil Casserole

Serves: 4-5
Prep time: 30 min

Ingredients:

1 lb ground beef

1 small onion, chopped

2 garlic cloves, crushed

1 cup dry green lentils

1 carrot, chopped

2 cups water

2 bay leaves

1 tsp dried oregano

1 tbsp paprika

1/2 tsp salt, black pepper, to taste

1/2 tsp cumin

3 tbsp extra virgin olive oil

Directions:

Heat the olive oil in a casserole over medium-high heat. Add the onion and carrot and sauté for 4-5 minutes. Add in the garlic and sauté for one more minute.

Add in the ground beef and cook for 4-5 minutes, stirring, until browned. Add the paprika, cumin, oregano, bay leaves, tomatoes, lentils and water.

Bring everything to a boil then reduce heat and simmer for 25 minutes, or until the beef is cooked through. Remove the bay leaves and serve.

Baked Cauliflower

Serves: 4
Prep time: 25 min

Ingredients:

1 small cauliflower, cut into florets

1 tbsp garlic powder

1 tsp paprika

salt, to taste

black pepper, to taste

4 tbsp extra virgin olive oil

Directions:

Combine olive oil, paprika, salt, pepper and garlic powder together.

Toss in the cauliflower florets and place in a baking dish in one layer. Bake in a preheated to 350F oven for 20 minutes or until golden.

Maple Roast Parsnip with Pear and Sage

Serves: 4
Prep time: 65 min

Ingredients:

5 parsnips, peeled, halved, cut into large wedges

2 large pears, cut into wedges

1 large onion, cut into wedges

1 tbsp garlic powder

1/3 cup fresh sage leaves

2 tbsp 100% pure maple syrup (unprocessed)

1/4 teaspoon dried chili flakes

4 tbsp extra virgin olive oil

Directions:

Preheat oven to 350F. Line 2 baking trays with baking paper. Place the parsnip, pear, onion, and sage on the prepared trays.

Combine the maple syrup, olive oil, garlic powder and dried chili flakes in a bowl.

Pour the maple mixture evenly over the parsnip mixture and gently toss to combine. Bake, turning halfway during cooking, for 1 hour or until the parsnip is golden and tender.

Balsamic Roasted Carrots and Baby Onions

Serves: 4
Prep time: 50 min

Ingredients:

2 bunches baby carrots, scrubbed, ends trimmed

10 small onions, peeled, halved

4 tbsp 100% pure maple syrup (unprocessed)

1 tsp thyme

2 tbsp extra virgin olive oil

Directions:

Preheat oven to 350F. Line a baking tray with baking paper.

Place the carrots, onion, thyme and oil in a large bowl and toss until well coated. Arrange carrots and onion, in a single layer, on the baking tray. Roast for 25 minutes or until tender.

Sprinkle over the maple syrup and vinegar and toss to coat. Roast for 25-30 minutes more or until vegetables are tender and caramelized. Season with salt and pepper to taste and serve.

Hearty Chicken Spinach Frittata

Serves: 4
Prep time: 30 min

Ingredients:

1 cup chicken, chopped finely

3-4 green onions, finely chopped

5 oz frozen chopped spinach, defrosted and excess moisture squeezed out

½ zucchini, peeled and shredded

1 large tomato, thinly sliced

2 tbsp fresh rosemary leaves, finely chopped

5 eggs

3 tbsp coconut milk

4 tbsp olive oil

Directions:

Grease a shallow casserole dish. Heat two tablespoons of olive oil in a frying pan and gently cook the chicken until almost cooked through. Add in the onions and garlic and cook for another minute. Set aside.

In the same pan, heat the remaining olive oil. Cook the zucchini and spinach, stirring constantly, until lightly cooked. Add in the chicken mixture, and combine everything well. Pour it all into the casserole.

In a medium bowl, whisk eggs, coconut milk and rosemary together. Pour over the top of the chicken and vegetable mixture, making sure that it covers it well. Lay the tomato slices on top.

Bake in a preheated to 360F oven for around 15 minutes, until set.

Chicken and Mushroom Frittata

Serves: 4
Prep time: 20 min

Ingredients:

1 cup roasted chicken meat, chopped

1 cup white mushrooms, chopped

½ onion, chopped

2 garlic cloves, chopped

1 large tomato, thinly sliced

1/2 tsp salt

1/2 tsp black pepper

1 tsp dried thyme

4 large eggs, beaten well

2 tbsp extra virgin olive oil

Directions:

Grease a shallow casserole dish. Heat two tablespoons of olive oil in a frying pan and gently cook the onions and garlic until onion is transparent. Add in the mushrooms, stir, and cook on medium-high heat for 3-4 minutes. Add in the chicken and combine everything well. Pour it into the casserole.

In a medium bowl, whisk eggs, coconut milk, salt, black pepper and thyme together. Pour over the top of the chicken and mushroom mixture, making sure that it covers it well. Lay the tomato slices on top. Bake in a preheated to 360F oven for around 15 minutes, until set.

Zucchini and Buckwheat Stew

Serves: 4-5
Prep time: 20 min

Ingredients:

1 cup buckwheat groats

1 ½ cups vegetable broth

1 onion, finely chopped

3 garlic cloves, chopped

4 zucchinis, peeled and diced

1 cup fresh dill, finely cut

3 tbsp extra virgin olive oil

salt, to taste

Directions:

Toast the buckwheat in a dry saucepan for about 2 minutes, stirring. Set aside.

In a deep saucepan, heat olive oil and gently sauté the onion and garlic for 1-2 minutes. Add the diced zucchinis and sauté for 5-6 minutes, stirring.

Add vegetable broth and bring to the boil. Stir in the toasted buckwheat, finely cut dill and salt to taste and simmer for 15-20 minutes.

Power Buckwheat Stew

Serves: 4-5
Prep time: 20 min

Ingredients:

1 cup buckwheat groats

1 cup vegetable broth or water

1 onion, chopped

1 potato, chopped

1 zucchini, peeled and chopped

1 tomato, diced

½ cup frozen corn kernels

½ cup frozen peas

½ cup black olives, halved, pitted

2 garlic cloves, minced

4 tbsp extra virgin olive oil

1 cup parsley, finely cut

Directions:

Toast the buckwheat in a dry saucepan for about 2 minutes, stirring; set aside.

In the same saucepan, heat olive oil and gently sauté the onion and garlic for a minute. Add in the green peas, potato, zucchini, corn, olives and cook, stirring for 3-4 minutes.

Add water or vegetable broth and bring to the boil. Stir in the diced tomato and the toasted buckwheat. Reduce heat, cover, and simmer for 10 minutes, stirring occasionally. Serve sprinkled with parsley and enjoy!

Curried Buckwheat with Raisins and Apples

Serves: 4-5
Prep time: 20 min

Ingredients:

1 cup buckwheat groats

1 3/4 cups vegetable broth

1 large apple, peeled and chopped

½ cup raisins

½ cup coarsely chopped almonds or walnuts

4-5 green onions, finely cut

1 tsp curry powder

¼ tsp ground turmeric

2 tbsp extra virgin olive oil

1 tbsp apple cider vinegar

salt and black pepper, to taste

Directions:

Toast the buckwheat in a dry saucepan for about 2 minutes, stirring. Boil the vegetable broth and add it gently to the buckwheat. Reduce heat, cover and simmer for 15 minutes, or until the buckwheat is tender. Remove from heat and fluff with a fork.

In a large bowl, toss together the apple, raisins, almonds and green onions. Add the cooked buckwheat and toss to combine.

In a small saucepan, warm the olive oil, curry and turmeric for 1-2 minutes. Remove from heat and let cool for 1 minute. Add the vinegar and pour this mixture over the buckwheat mixture. Stir until all ingredients are well coated.

Quick Buckwheat Chili

Serves: 4-5
Prep time: 20-25 min

Ingredients:

1 cup buckwheat groats

1 ¾ cups vegetable broth

1 large onion, finely cut

3 cloves garlic, chopped

1 green bell pepper, chopped

1 can diced tomatoes

1 can mixed beans, well rinsed and drained

1 tbsp paprika

1 tsp chili powder

1 tsp ground cumin

2 tbsp extra virgin olive oil

Directions:

Toast the buckwheat in a dry saucepan for about 2 minutes, stirring, then set aside.

In a large soup pot or casserole dish, heat the oil over medium heat. Add the onion, bell pepper and garlic and sauté until softened, about 3 minutes. Stir in the chili powder, cumin and paprika and sauté for another minute. Add the buckwheat and stir to combine well.

Stir in the tomatoes, beans and vegetable broth.

Bring to a boil then reduce heat to low and simmer, covered, for about 20 minutes. Serve sprinkled with fresh coriander.

Eggplant and Chickpea Stew

Serves 4
Prep time: 25 min

Ingredients:

2 medium eggplants, peeled and diced

1 large onion, finely cut

2 garlic cloves, chopped

1 15 oz can chickpeas, drained

1 cup canned tomatoes, undrained, diced

1 cup green olives

1 tbsp paprika

1 tsp cumin

3 tbsp olive oil

salt and pepper, to taste

1 cup parsley leaves, very finely cut, to serve

Directions:

Heat olive oil in a deep casserole dish and sauté onions and garlic. Add paprika and cumin, stir, and sauté for 2-3 minutes, or until the onions have softened. Add the eggplant cubes, tomatoes, olives and chickpeas and bring to a boil.

Lower heat and simmer, covered, for 20 minutes, or until the eggplant is tender. Season with salt and black pepper to taste, uncover, and simmer 4-5 minutes until the liquid evaporates.

Serve sprinkled with parsley.

Spicy Chickpea and Spinach Stew

Serves: 4
Prep time: 20 min

Ingredients:

1 onion, chopped

3 garlic cloves, chopped

1 15 oz can chickpeas, drained and rinsed

1 15 oz can tomatoes, diced and undrained

1 1 lb bag baby spinach

a handful of blanched almonds

½ cup vegetable broth

1 tbsp hot chili paste

½ tsp cumin

salt and pepper, to taste

Directions:

Heat the olive oil in a large saucepan over medium-high heat. Gently the sauté onion and garlic for 4-5 minutes, or until tender. Add spices and stir. Add in the chickpeas, tomatoes, almonds and broth.

Bring to a boil, then reduce heat to low and simmer, partially covered, for 10 minutes. Add the chili paste and spinach to the pot and stir until the spinach wilts.

Remove from heat and season with salt and pepper to taste.

Moroccan Chickpea Stew

Serves: 4-5
Prep time: 20 min

Ingredients:

1 onion, chopped

3 garlic cloves, chopped

2 large carrots, chopped

2 sweet potatoes, peeled and chopped

4-5 dates, pitted and chopped

1 cup spinach, chopped

1 15 oz can tomatoes, diced and undrained

1 15 oz can chickpeas, rinsed and drained

1 cup vegetable broth

1 tbsp ground cumin

½ tsp chili powder

½ tsp ground turmeric

½ teaspoon salt

3 tbsp extra virgin olive oil

½ cup chopped cilantro, to serve

grated lemon zest, to serve

Directions:

Heat the olive oil in a large saucepan over medium-high heat. Gently sauté onion, garlic and carrots for 4-5 minutes, or until tender. Add all spices and stir. Stir in all other ingredients except the spinach.

Bring to a boil, cover, reduce heat, and simmer for 20 minutes, or until the potatoes are tender. Add in the spinach, stir and cook it until it wilts.

Serve over brown rice or quinoa and top with chopped cilantro and lemon zest.

Baked Falafels

Serves: 7
Prep time: 20-30 min

Ingredients:

1 can chickpeas, drained and rinsed

1 small carrot, cut

1 onion, cut

2 garlic cloves, minced

½ cup fresh parsley, finely cut

¼ cup almond flour

¼ cup tahini

1/4 cup extra virgin olive oil

2-3 tbsp lemon juice

2 tsp cumin (or to taste)

1 tsp salt

black pepper, to taste

Directions:

Blend the carrots, chickpeas, onion and garlic in a food processor until completely minced. When it turns to a smooth paste, add in parsley and transfer to a large mixing bowl. Stir in the remaining ingredients.

Using a large tablespoon form batter into burgers. Bake in a preheated to 375 F oven until golden.

Chickpea, Rice and Mushroom Stew

Serves: 4-5
Prep time: 20-30 min

Ingredients:

1 15 oz can chickpeas, drained

1 large onion, finely cut

2 cups mushrooms, chopped

2 carrots, chopped

1 15 oz can tomatoes, diced, undrained

1/3 cup rice, washed

1 cup vegetable broth

4 tbsp extra virgin olive oil

1 tsp oregano

1 tbsp paprika

1 cup fresh parsley, finely cut

1 tbsp sugar

Directions:

In a deep, heavy-bottomed saucepan, heat olive oil and gently sauté the onion and carrots for 4-5 minutes, stirring constantly. Add in paprika, chickpeas, rice, mushrooms, tomatoes, sugar and vegetable broth and stir again.

Season with salt, oregano, ground black pepper and bring to the boil. Cover, reduce heat, and simmer for about 20 minutes, stirring from time to time.

Sprinkle with parsley, simmer for a minute more and serve.

Chickpea, Leek and Olive Stew

Serves: 4-5
Prep time: 20 min

Ingredients:

5 cups sliced leeks

25-30 black olives, pitted and halved

1 15 oz can chickpeas, drained

½ cup water

1 tbsp tomato paste

4 tbsp extra virgin olive oil

salt and black pepper, to taste

Directions:

In a deep baking dish, heat olive oil and sauté the leeks for 2-3 minutes. Add in the chickpeas and olives. Dissolve the tomato paste in half a cup of warm water and add it to the chickpeas.

Season with black pepper and bake in a preheated to 350F oven for 20-25 minutes. Serve and enjoy!

Easy Homemade Baked Beans

Serves: 4-5
Prep time: soaking 7-8 hrs, cooking 90 min

Ingredients:

1 cup white beans

3 ½ cups water

1 onion, chopped

2 red peppers, chopped

1 tomato, diced

1 carrot, chopped

3 tbsp extra virgin olive oil

1 tbsp paprika

2 tbsp dried mint

½ cup fresh parsley

1 tsp salt

Directions:

Wash the beans and soak them in water overnight. In the morning discard the water, pour 3 cups of fresh water and cook the beans for an hour or until soft but not falling apart. Discard the water again and set the beans aside.

Heat olive oil in a ovenproof dish and sauté onions, peppers, tomato and carrot. Add paprika and mint and stir in the beans. Add half a cup of water, season with salt and bake in a preheated to 350F oven for 30 minutes. Serve warm.

Baked Bean and Rice Casserole

Serves: 4-5
Prep time: 30 min

Ingredients:

2 15 oz cans white or red beans, drained

1 cup water or vegetable broth

2/3 cup rice

2 onions, chopped

½ bunch parsley, finely cut

7-8 fresh mint leaves, finely cut

3 tbsp extra virgin olive oil

1 tbsp paprika

½ tsp black pepper

1 tsp salt

Directions:

Heat olive oil in an ovenproof casserole dish and gently sauté the chopped onions for 1-2 minutes. Stir in paprika and rice and cook, stirring constantly for another minute.

Add in the beans with a cup of water or vegetable broth, season with salt and black pepper, stir in mint and parsley and bake in a preheated to 350F oven for 20 minutes.

Green Pea and Rice Casserole

Serves: 4-5
Prep time: 20 min

Ingredients:

1 onion, chopped

1 1 lb bag frozen peas

3 garlic cloves, chopped

3-4 mushrooms, chopped

2/3 cup white rice

1 cup water

4 tbsp extra virgin olive oil

3 tbsp dill, finely cut

salt and black pepper, to taste

Directions:

In a deep ovenproof casserole dish, heat olive oil and sauté the onions, garlic and mushrooms for 2-3 minutes. Add in the rice and cook, stirring constantly for 1 minute.

Add in a cup of warm water and the frozen peas, stir and bake in a preheated to 350F oven for 20 minutes. Sprinkle with dill, bake for 2-3 more minutes and serve.

Breakfast and Dessert Recipes

Hearty Quinoa and Spinach Breakfast Casserole

Serves: 4
Prep time: 30 min

Ingredients:

1 cup cooked quinoa

3-4 spring onions, finely chopped

5 oz frozen chopped spinach, thawed and squeezed dry

½ zucchini, peeled and shredded

5 eggs

1/2 coconut milk

4 tbsp extra virgin olive oil

salt and black pepper, to taste

Directions:

In a large bowl combine eggs, coconut milk, salt and pepper.

In a deep casserole dish heat the olive oil. Cook the onions, zucchini and spinach, stirring constantly, until lightly cooked. Add in the quinoa and combine everything well. Pour the egg mixture over and bake in a preheated to 350F oven for 20 minutes.

Applesauce Pancakes

Serves: 10 pancakes
Prep time: 20 min

Ingredients:

4 large eggs

2/3 cup unsweetened homemade apple sauce

1/3 cup almond meal

3 tbsp ground flaxseed

1 tsp baking powder

1/2 tsp cinnamon

2 tbsp maple syrup

Directions:

Whisk eggs in a small bowl. Combine with applesauce, maple syrup and cinnamon.

In another bowl, combine almond meal, baking powder and ground flaxseed. Add to the wet ingredients; do not overmix.

Spray a pan with coconut oil spray and heat to low/medium . Once pan is fully heated, spoon in a tablespoon of batter.

Cook for about 3-4 minutes each side, or until firm enough to flip.

Super Easy Blueberry Pancakes

Serves: 10 pancakes
Prep time: 10 min

Ingredients:

2 ripe bananas, mashed

3 large eggs

1 tbsp almond meal

3 tbsp ground flaxseed

1 tsp baking powder

1 tsp vanilla extract

coconut oil for the pan

a pinch of salt

2 tbsp blueberries

Directions:

In a bowl, whisk eggs with a pinch of salt.

Mash bananas with a fork and add to the eggs. Stir in blueberries, flaxseed, almond meal and baking powder.

Spray a pan with coconut oil spray and heat to low/medium. Once pan is fully heated spoon in a tablespoon of batter.

Let the pancake set for a minute or flip it when the center starts to bubble.

Serve immediately, topped with fresh fruit, a bit of maple syrup or agave.

Raspberry Muffins

Serves: 12
Prep time: 20 min

Ingredients:

3 eggs

2 1/2 cups almond meal

1 tbsp ground flaxseed

1/2 tsp baking soda

1/2 cup raw honey

1/4 cup melted coconut oil

3 tbsp lemon juice

1 tsp vanilla extract

1 cup raspberries

Directions:

Preheat oven to 325 degrees.

In a bowl, mix together the dry ingredients. Combine the wet ingredients in another bowl then add too dry mixture. Do not overmix.

Spoon batter into prepared muffin tin; bake 20 minutes or until tops start to brown and a toothpick inserted into a muffin comes out clean.

Raw Brownie Bites

Serves: 10-12
Prep time: 5 min

Ingredients:

1 cup walnuts

1 cup pitted dates

2 tbsp cranberries

1 tbsp flaxseed

1 tbsp sesame seeds

1 pinch of salt

1 tsp vanilla extract

1/3 cup unsweetened cocoa powder

Directions:

Combine all ingredients in a food processor and process until everything is well mixed together.

Drop heaping tablespoon amounts of the batter onto a prepared baking sheet and sprinkle with shredded coconut.

Allow cookies to chill in the refrigerator for at least 60 minutes and serve.

Zucchini Breakfast Smoothie

Serves: 2
Prep time: 2-3 min

Ingredients:

1 frozen banana

1 cup orange juice

½ zucchini, peeled and chopped

2 apricots, chopped

1 tbsp chia seeds

Directions:

Combine all ingredients in a high speed blender and blend until smooth.

About the Author

Alissa Grey is a fitness and nutrition enthusiast who loves to teach people about losing weight and feeling better about themselves. She lives in a small French village in the foothills of a beautiful mountain range with her husband, three teenage kids, two free spirited dogs, and various other animals.

Alissa is incredibly lucky to be able to cook and eat natural foods, mostly grown nearby, something she's done since she was a teenager. She enjoys yoga, running, reading, hanging out with her family, and growing organic vegetables and herbs.

If you want to see other delicious and healthy family recipes that she has published you can check out her Author Page on Amazon.

Printed in Great Britain
by Amazon